Mercy Said,
Justice Gone

Drawing on his background in law, David Shannon playfully deconstructs what it means to be human in the 21st century, delving in particular into experiences of disability and dislocation. Written in the style of a play, we are invited to go on a journey of witness to a place "where no light shines," and asked to reckon with our own humility and humanity in the face of strife, lost kindness, and an almost total lack of sympathy. This book will break your heart and mend it back together again, all in one fell swoop.

—Andrea Rexilius, Director of the Creative Writing programme at Regis University in Denver

We enter David Shannon's *Mercy Said* as witnesses warned that justice is gone, and through a beauty and play with language and form, his poetry becomes the catastrophic injuries that tear us apart: addiction, disability, poverty, homelessness, and the doctors who slate us to die because it's easier than fixing us. This collection also becomes the stitches that sew us back together, the nourishment that feeds us, the blanket that wraps us up for the night. Through his writing, Shannon is an advocate for the sick, the discarded, the forgotten, the euthanized. His poetry will wound, destroy, resurrect… keep us "less than well and more than ill," and our "minds above the curtains and grounded by the balls" in complete mental disorder. This collection is "paper on our jugular," an unapologetic pressure sore you'll want to pick at until it looks nothing like the reality exposed here.

—Shannon Malloy, Poet

The five-act parable *Mercy Said*, is both a critique and contemplation of what happens when justice and mercy are declared in order to negate compassion. In poetic form, David Shannon explores the paradoxes of the violent use of so-called justice and mercy in current political discourses and amidst social fissures of disability. In the parables and poems of *Mercy Said*, we see the profound intersections of disability with poverty, vulnerability, and addiction.

David Shannon, CM, OOnt (b. 1963) is a Canadian disability and human rights activist, lawyer, university lecturer, author, and adventurer. He is most recently co-editor (with Dr. Jaro Kotalik) of *Medical Assistance in Dying (MAID) in Canada: Key Interdisciplinary Perspectives* [Vol. 1] (Springer, 2023) and *Medical Assistance in Dying (MAID) in Canada: Trends and Consequences* [Vol. 2] (Springer, 2025).

Pandora Poetica

Volume 1, Pedro A. Sandín-Fremaint,
Hello, Stranger: Thresholds of the Unfamiliar
(Pandora Press, 2025)

Volume 2, David Shannon,
Mercy Said, Justice Gone: A Parable in Five Acts
(Pandora Press, 2025)

Volume 3, Otto Selles
Matins
(Pandora Press, 2025)

Mercy Said, Justice Gone

A Parable in Five Acts

David Shannon

PANDORA
PRESS

MERCY SAID, JUSTICE GONE: A PARABLE IN FIVE ACTS
DAVID SHANNON
ISBN-13: 978-1-77873-032-0

Book design, cover design, and editing by Maxwell Kennel.
Cover image: Meghan Harder, "Dutch Interior" (installation detail) 2021.

Table of Contents

Act I. We Touch the Gate

Act II. Visit the Imprisoned

Act III. A Grieving Illness

Act IV. Mercy None

Act V. Fair Again

Epilogue

Narrators

Roo

Ree

The Chorus

Act I

We Touch The Gate

Mercy Said, Justice Gone

(Chorus enters)

Welcome, we will wander as we touch the gate.[1]

Is this the present, or are we lost

writhing in contemporaneous debate?

Blink-   -a century is not then long.[2]

What happens with mercy said, but justice gone[3]

---

[1] Dante Allighieri, The Inferno, Canto III, Through me to the city dolorous lies the way, Who pass through me shall pains eternal prove, Through me are reached the people lost for aye…Ye who make entrance, every hope resign!

[2] MD FAHAD HOSSAIN, *Time and Narrative in Samuel Beckett's Waiting for Godot and Endgame;* The concept of time as linear progression is the lie in which Beckett's characters are trapped. Rather than act as a vehicle of mobility, Time is the penultimate source of immobility. It is the tragic reflection of the fallen state of man, exalted paradoxically by debasement and disenfranchisemt.

[3] William Shakespeare, King Lear, Act IV, Scene vi

> Through tattered clothes great vices do appear
> Robes and furred gowns hide all.
> Plate sin with gold and the strong lance of justice hurtless breaks.
> Arm it in rags, a pigmy's straw does pierce it.;
> William Shakespeare, Macbeth, Act IV, Scene iii
> As justice, verity, temp'rance, stableness,
> Bounty, perseverance, mercy, lowliness,
> Devotion, patience, courage, fortitude,
> I have no relish of them, but abound
> In the division of each several crime,
> Acting in many ways.
> William Shakespeare, Measure for Measure, Act I, Scene III,

to bring a fetid time of mercy none? [4]

A consecration without the tender or the dead,

hunger for an imprisoned bed,

tented winter without blankets, for no one fed,

a grieving illness ignoring true love led,

staying satiated until she's dead. [5]

I see your discontent, [6] and if it does offend,

Liberty plucks justice by the nose;
The baby beats the nurse,
and quite athwart Goes all decorum.

[4] William Shakespeare, The Tempest, Act V, Epilogue ll. 15-20

And my ending is despair,
 Unless I be relieved by prayer,
 Which pierces so that it assaults
 Mercy itself, and frees all faults.
The Merchant of Venice, Act IV, Scene I
The quality of mercy is not strained;
It droppeth as the gentle rain from heaven
Upon the place beneath. It is twice blest;
It blesseth him that gives and him that takes:

[5] See: *The Seven Works of Mercy*, a work by Michelangelo Merisi da Caravaggio circa 1607. Inspired by: Matthew 35:36, [35] For I was hungry and you gave me something to eat, I was thirsty and you gave me something to drink, I was a stranger and you invited me in, [36] I needed clothes and you clothed me, I was sick and you looked after me, I was in prison and you came to visit me.

[6] William Shakespeare, Richard III, Act 1, LL. 1,

Now is the winter of our discontent

Journey here,[7] perhaps love you'll find.

Or, check each sentence[8] to feel the flush

of fear for difference now in your brain.

Then, the foul will be fair again.[9]

---

[7] William Shakespeare, A Midsummer Night's Dream, Act V, Scene i

> If we shadows have offended,
> Think but this and all is mended.
> That you have but slumbered here
> While these visions did appear.
> And this weak and idle theme,
> No more yielding but a dream.
> Gentles, do not reprehend.
> If you pardon, we will mend.

[8] Hossain, *Ibid*, An obvious thing about a dramatic narrative is that it presents us with a kind of model of time while building a relationship between a text and its reading. The experience of reading accords with a tensed conception of time which is subjective. This tensed conception of time only gives the existence to the present, blocking the view of time in which past and present co-exist simultaneously. For this reason, while reading we experience the past as a quasi-present, and not because there is any ontological difference between fiction and life. Every written text has a dormant future which waits to be actualized by the reading.

[9] William Shakespeare, Macbeth Act 1, scene 3,

> So foul and fair a day I have not seen

Wander Bodily

Chorus

Are you who you thought you were?
Wander in this makeshift body.
Answer purpose pleasantly.
What was always was what where.

A Street with no Dead End

I was born on a street with no dead end
Born on energy from the brown grass mowed
Meant for escape on an elastic road
I'm a creature on concrete creating a home

When living in London, we're eating Italian
...Espresso strong
matching mother's sauce
tasting momentary Barolo

We wander full wet on Rainbow Beach
finding foam floating
on the energy end

Queen Street Subway Was Fixed

Future forward subway ran.

Rain from asphalted
dripping shoe toes
running flowed down steps
 sliding seepage to
the wheelchair stroller cycle
ramp under the
jack hammered crack.

Fluorescent florid tile dripped
from window showing
fast flash tunnel darkness.
Doors shuttered by shoulders
pressed in quiet eyes
dying to vomit from dying.

A Day At The Office

On the harbour

          when waves of rain will turn a face

you promise I'll be anchored

I

      float

             where

splinters come

                 from solid root

as the glass building enters me.

Harbour Town Tour

overpass to soiled
pebbled mud shouldered drive
    always is always

stop sign red says, 'doing coke'
    gray deadwood grave reads, "Forest"
splinters wait for wind

gold grass splits asphalt
    Bent fence cordons staff parking
        Job cemetery

Nylon domed homes
    Plaid shirts slide and dry beside
    zippered sleeping bag

At The Door

When he calls for a burger
He is not a beggar at the door
When he asks for 20 bucks
He is not a beggar at the door
When he shows with sandals bent toes slipped in sidewalk slide
He is not a beggar at the door
When he calls at night and I remind him of the time
He is not a beggar at the door
When the guardian will not buy a bicycle for his absent son
He is not a beggar at the door
When he weeps because he has no soap
He is not a beggar at the door
When an inhale cracks the quiet, the voices beg no more

Act II

"visit the imprisoned"

Chorus

Movement Without Muscle

When silence is said without a word.
When noise is made with no one left.
When freedom reaches flightless bird.
When action is promised with nothing done.
When night is midday for no one heard.

Then response is swallowed by ubiquitous wave.
Then wait for hours when minutes suffice
Then internal belief lifts forms for what's left
Then fiction controls a mystery voiced
Then silence is said for presumption of worth

I Chose

I chose to become a patient because
I had never experienced systemization, structure,
tiled walls, faux art, incurably
perfect antiseptic residue,
or magnificent absence of self.

This is my anchored cruise ship.

There are so many beautiful
moments
to let irreverence speed beyond rules,
or open my heart and tongue
to stories of fluids,
ooze, and dark strange crudities to
strangers.
With chin protruding
and thoughtful whispering pupils,
they listen
embracing an industrialization of corporeal degeneration.

My mind rises above the curtains as
they keep me grounded by my balls.

The grandeur of being a being
where discharge
has two distinct meanings.
One to look inward
excusing you from the outward,
the other
immediate extrication.

That was my mission –
the plot to my drama.

Slide within the land of the folding bed
Avoid a forced exit to
the parking lot
where:
I am a shadow in a window;
Hope directed by an intersection;
A pedestrian crowded by sewage.

Half Human

I

Let me speak.   Let me leave.
Shut the fuck up.   Shut the fuck up.
Restraints.   Fuck you.
I left my cat behind.

I have bills to pay.
Call my lawyer.

I have to get out.
I'm here as an accident.
Sister called the cops.
Stars explode.

You're a corpse.

Doctor, you're in shambles.
Untie my legs.
Hope is gone and solace none[8]
The white heat medicine is a mistake.
My sister called the cops.

Let me out tomorrow

Or I'll be set on fire

II

medicalized bodies

        take human form

                                in a
                        psychiatric world

                choice without legal recourse
      Obscure   powerless   silence

 'incapacity'
for a scratch card lottery.
You're a half humanity:

                debris on a highway motel table top;
                a jurisprudential amorality,

the irrelevance of compromised cogency.
A half humanity.

R. v. Human

BETWEEN

THE KING

-AND-

YOU

a) Between any day and now someone will say you harassed, assaulted, entered, ate, became present.

b) That you in any municipality everywhere anytime did unlawfully presume to orderly function possessing your allegedly disordered mind.

c) That an intellectual disability is not a medical or adjudicative compliment.

Proceedings will proceed in preservation of liberty, equality, security, to guarantee a *Constitution* constituted of residential and hospital options *Chartering* freedom for being less than well and more than ill notwithstanding the above-mentioned serious offences.

1. **The DETAILED STATEMENT OF THE SPECIFIC FACTUAL BASIS PROVING CONSCIENTOUS GOVERNMENTAL RIGHTS GUARANTEES ABSENTING YOUR DISABILITY**

a. EVERY HUMAN HERE IS promised freedoms on account of mental disorder. A promise of process.

b. EVERY HUMAN HERE IS handed handcuffs, ankle chains, locked to bed. In carceral in incarceration restrained from wellness in criminalized illness.

c. HERE, shackles are liberty. Delays pick up process potent for your orderly attachment to the metal slipped around your wrist, pulling to your chest, linking to your foot, harnessing your hip

d. HERE put into in into in into inhumane in your bed chain with observant eyeballs held in a circular scene squinting to your breast from those men: in black polyester, booted, shoulder patched guardians of the metal rope you hang from in your room, protectors of intrusion, while the gold thread on shoulder glistens as you open from a sleep. What is in their pants while you are in your sheets?

e. HERE, singular simple slit of window to Canadian winter backyard landscape bordering hospital parking lot gives gray gray gray penetration to the floor tight to acne scarred cinderblocks painted pale waiting for your stencil sketched paper of brilliant pocks of color as the blocks on blocks are built around your bones.

Bird On Canvas

On witnessing 'Thunderbird' by Norval Morrisseau

Bird on canvas

          is this your fate?

Bulge

          on back and broken wing

twisted feet   reach

          split   spit

of separate feathers

          to trap you flat forever

Painted   brilliant pasted-

          donation fed

homage

          to butter of a benefactor's bread

I see distraction in your jaundiced eye

        pit and balls

vibrant pale

        so those who purchase are regaled

Is it 4 o'clock?

Pulling from the safety
severed long ago
There is
Sound of rooftop
Faucet
Silence from the hall
shuffle at my door
Flying through my popcorn ceiling
As I
retreat
to website purchase relief
YouTube panacea
confirm the temperature on my wine fridge
Is it 4 o'clock?

Wandering to my cat I would like to know what he knows because I have
not reclined in the window scratched at the screen licked from a bowl or
jumped on a cluttered table for a very long time.

Only What Was Stolen

Sting of a heater on my vein throbs close.

A hollow hum.

Noises of a disappearance.

Pores listen.

Pulse opens

with dust fallen follicles.

No criminality

(only what was stolen from me).

But, flowers land in forests.

Day of Sleep Night and Day

I

Chorus Lead

Dear Roo,

Checking to see how you're holding up in your little condo you call home.

I know the pace of non pace.

II

Dear Roo,

I feel the drips on snow ice asphalt
falling on mould in my eye
waiting for popcorn ceiling to join
my guts on paper
plum sauce on fingers
tongue on last night's basmati
the lamp post swirls
Step on carpet.
Floor forward.
Clock ticks
Turn, read, watch TV, text, Safari.
Repeat.
A cheap watch is my friend and commandant
The dichotomous day of sleep night and day
entreating the concrete
propelling me to perpetuity

Act III

A Grieving Illness

Scene i

Fragility Has Lost Kindness

Mercy when fragility has lost kindness.
Mercy when an illness may be who we are.
Mercy when the desperate are left loveless.
Mercy without medicine or rest.

For The Lady who is Erasing Wounds

On witnessing Pieta by:
Michelangelo di Lodovico Buonarroti Simoni

I see your cement shoes.
                    Pieta
            Saintly lady

of decay.

You raised flesh

            erased wounds
            when fingers fell.

In negation   why inclusion?
        Is love the resurrection from your rooted tower?

But we feel paper on our jugular
where mobility is power,

                            Pieta.

Grounded Absence

I

Stare, talk with its usual circularity. Be.
She's half present, and quietly being there,
be present.
grounded in the absence of pretense that
fragile dementia brings
stare out her window from that empty room.
The street sits there
elongated shadows of the nearly popped leaves
little comfort as wet twigs dangled strip-like peaceful non life.

II

      Her figure bent. Nails elongated, near translucent. Hands white, white. The hunchback over her shuffle made me thankful every moment her gait did not tip her onto nose. The repetition of discussion of her kids of her family seemed acute.

An oversized white sweater with Kleenex hooked upward, folding, teetering - a shabbiness that bit hard.

      I brought groceries. Not love.

A Shattered Window Where No Light Shines

I

Microwave pork sits sour and dry

call came
Mom fell, hit chair
Paramedic checked
Fuck

sufferings transpose to memory

clinging to fear in my translucent tears

A blanket for cold

A cough is calling.... "hi"

a false salve for the living

Sleep   sleep   sleep

II

Her jaw lock flakes as the air penetrates

eyes hold distance as fate

evaporates

the hour has no more fading whispers

(Amber walls have allowed the gray sky into the ceiling.

Light was where a moment ago?)

A shake, a wake, for a head that does not turn

glasses that do not see.

Watching mom die

is a shattered window where no light shines.

Each crack filled with sadness.

An ancient teacup where stained veins pulsate nowhere.

Seven Severed Splintered

Seven pelvic fractures

           Splinter nerves
           alive to tear your torso.

                wait in time's irrelevance
where veins flow spears and spikes,
evaporating in the immolation
descending from the sun

rippling cuts from chest to thigh
a suspension
           trapping you in suicide

Special Residential Something

Your call fucked up my gnocchi milkshake special
I was watching a plate /creamy/ wet/stagnant.   A delivery special

I answered.   Guess that makes you special.
The specialist saw you with 16 hours notice. That's a drive thru medical
special.

Experts become a specialist when knowing control of other people's
schedules.
 Then you can thank them for advising on your crisis.   That
makes them special.

Your something would only be something if it were special.

 I forgot about the group of pensive residents. Following parental
specialist: desperate- hoping to be special. A new degree to become a
specialist.

Toing and froing babble babble, hush-hush, pencils, pencils wide-eyed,
clipboard touching, red cheek, pursed lip, kiss circling the expert's anus
(and, this is not an unfinished erotic tryptich).

You sit.
They sit, letting you dream of a modicum of material equality,
sometimes-   but only if their wisdom is possessed of gravity.

Beware the sit down.

You will be stared through to the back of your skull burning the top of the
head rest behind you, leaving a hole in the wall as they exit.

You naked.

Good to know you have something irremediable.   If you did not,
they would not be so special.

Your Creation Preserving A Memory Lost

The frame on the wall holds
your child hand. Clay makes a coast on paper watery blue
Rubber worms in a plaster tomb struggle.
Your creation preserving a memory lost.
                Echoes of laughter clouded on air.
Butterflies floating.   Hollowed by glass

Your ashes boxed   wait in tin and glass
Clasped in a locket of gold, it holds
your story soon to return to the air.
Silent on earth, floating in blue.
Youth over wisdom. We all are lost-
discovering what caused your childhood struggle

You shrouded abuse with inevitable struggle
Bones and emotion pounded like glass.
Brought to a host where you lost
and degraded life holds
adults grabbing your limbs turning blue.
Over then over   you   hoping for air.

You, born begging for air.
Small lungs made to struggle
gasped at your future boxed until blue
then finding escape in an inhale of piped glass.
Memories faded. Nothing to hold.
Those rubber framed butterflies now lost.

Recovery came after surgery lost.
You quietly serving those with no heir.
Giving to peers reliving similar stories held.
Finding your heritage.   Exposing their struggle.

Bringing strength through expression, not emotional glass.
Breaking the bonds of limbs once blue.

But now I am quiet. Paper mache fading from blue.
Your heart fought with its valve until it was lost
That frame hides cracks detached in the glass.
My guilt thick for ignoring your air.
Failures in love left you to struggle.
Gone are your gifts to no longer hold

Subtlety surrounds the struggle of grief.
Our bond rooted in plaster where
ethereal air is rubber in glass.

Antagonistic Rain

I cannot touch the vapor in my nostrils
Nor illumination on photos in a frame
My diaphragm in a memory

Ode To A Pressure Sore

You are a patient when you test the world while wearing SCI[10]

pressure
Severely ulcers lives
of SCI-
pressure
Severely ulcers lives

When chasing action, attending to nutrition, actualizing with socialization, and discovering equanimity through meditation you have a three out of five chance of discovering that pressure ulcers continue to impact the lives of spinal cord injury (SCI) patients severely.

Press

 Negating dignity is its own reward.

Pressure ulcers must be accurately staged according to National Pressure Ulcer Advisory recommendations before treatment design. An individuation stated is the best identification.

Press

                              You ignored the silent friend purchasing
flesh:

---

[10] Braided with the abstract from the article: "Spinal cord injury pressure ulcer treatment: an experience-based approach." *Sunn G. Phys Med Rehabil Clin N Am.* 2014 Aug;25(3):671-80, ix. doi: 10.1016/j.pmr.2014.05.002. SCI=Spinal Cord Injury

Red? not red
Broken tissue bits? Benign
Pain diminished when diverted

Pick your healthy binges. The first priority in treatment of pressure ulcers is offloading. You will need to find new fun in bed.

Press

Ligamental tightening in supine

contractures

creates a rigid composure
quiet Knees
unstretched
muscles silent
while you heal.

Intact skin ulcers may be treated with noncontact nonthermal low-frequency ultrasound like a day at the spa with pedicures and rosacea removal.

Press

Scheduling medical priorities replaces jobs
Consuming love
In a void-uncertain

Press

Superficial pressure ulcers may be treated with a combination of collagenase and foam dressings because they are the latest in bedrest fashion. Such isolation is emerald clothing.

Press

Infected heat to touch?
Visitors bring buoyancy
to the weighted awakening message

Press

Deeper pressure ulcers warrant negative-pressure wound therapy dressings along with biologic adjuncts to fill in wound depth. You will measure tunnels in tissue. Meet new nursing faces while wishing their uninvited family story familiarity is soon forgotten.

Press

Discovery and treatment of osteomyelitis is a high priority when initially evaluating pressure ulcers. The Mayo Clinic website says, this is an infection in a bone reaching it by traveling through the bloodstream, spreading from nearby tissue or beginning in the bone itself if an injury exposes the bone to germs.

This will allow you to meet very interesting infectious disease experts who have been bored since Covid changed.

Press

Surgical intervention must always be considered.

Where dark new lines of scars soon to be pink will hold drainage tubes for one week.

Air filled mattresses and medication with dressing changes will be your home where you take that rest.

Elusive rest.

Breathe.

Breathe.

Silent stars.
Just breathe

the my inside
reaches your window pane

while it waits with winter twigs in the grey air.

Act IV

a fetid time of mercy none
consecration without the tender or the dead,

Would That You Were Dead

Scene i: Chorus

Would that you should be dead
by a morally eroded soul who said,
"The dissolution of difference is an
exaltation to presented autonomy,"
suffusing its meaning swimming in
the ignorance of post-reason reality
where disgust honours a preference
 for dislodging dislike through self-destruction.
expertly absenting medical complexity
for an invocation of feigned mercy.
A consecration in a totalitarian time
of opinion for a subjective society.
A negation where questions are erased
by non thought for majoritarian faith.

Roo

CONSECRATED MERCY

I

Come gather in the hallway. See our display.
There- Hitler- in this picture penned
a note to his citizens extending
endings to any disability
 through provision of these powers
to physicians with their best discretion.
A consecration of a merciful end
to their fellow German. 325,000 deaths
three years hence were the ally's ally.
Canada rescinded prohibitions
against physician assisted death,
regulating ethos by bypassing
 illness in dying until finding favour
for said services to the poor and oppressed.

What questions are left?

Note: "Consecrated Mercy" integrates direct quotes from the Supreme Court case, and partial English translation of Hitler's letter in bold.

II

ENTER CHORUS

Bouhler and Dr. Brandt ARE instructed,	prohibition prohib ibition
under their responsibility,	against physician-assisted dying[11]
to extend the powers of physicians	violates the rights
to be designated	violates
liberty	
in particular	violates
in such a way	security of the person
that,	violates autonomy
at human discretion,	violates quality of life[12]
violates	
terminally ill persons	suffering
can be consecrated mercy	intolerable.[13] ...

---

[11] The court used the softer language "physician-assisted dying". They did not offer such loaded lingo as "euthanasia, mercy killing, or Dr. death". When the words of the plaintiff were utilized by the court, the defense had to have known that their argument was dead on arrival. No need to turn to page 2.

[12] What about equality? The Supreme Court was asked to provide a substantive equality analysis, and refused. That is the vulnerability. The history of forced sterilization, institutionalization in the name of therapy- ignored. The unemployability when there is a disability, insecure housing, diminishment of agency ignored while they lay as precursors to long-term care COVID eldercide.

[13] Who is suffering? Define suffering. Where is there palliative care?

Consecrated mercy

in the event   -
physicians
of a critical assessment   better able to provide overall end-of-life
treatment
of their state of illness

vulnerability can be
consecrated mercy

extend the powers of physicians
powers of physicians
powers of physicians

Mercy
Mercy

- no compelling evidence that a permissive regime in Canada
would result in a "practical slippery slope"

mercy

- risks associated with physician-assisted death

Mercy

can be limited through a carefully designed
and monitored system of safeguards.

Mercy

- We should not lightly assume
that the regulatory regime will function defectively,

Mercy

- nor should we assume that other criminal sanctions

Mercy

against the taking of lives will prove impotent against abuse.

MERCY

"human life
should not be
depreciated
by allowing life
to be taken".
… an animating social value
rather than a
description
of the specific
object of the prohibition.

MERCY

an angel's obsolescence

Cheetah pities human in the chase
walking is an angel's obsolescence

I do not know how I go

as language creeps in my sleep
shock and bliss,

impossible to hold.

I hold the dream I am

day obstructs.

Coffee clouds my eyes

Morning thoughts of day

Blood
heaves to my nose

A cold vapor morning
holds in haze

I think of next

Leave bed

Memory evaporates

A curiosity

    -by noon

a dementia

       bliss

          impossible

A Compulsive Connection

ENTER CHORUS

The professor read a poem- core curriculum
choose a wheelchair, with an injury
Thank a friend for death, "Push me from a cliff,"
he said, pacing, seeking post-PhD relevance.

An orator promoting merciful
university sanctioned suicide.
This thought aloud and normalized.
Silence from the classmates as their stares
proliferated from peripheral glare.
Afraid to look at her directly while he read.

Was it her attraction to the poem?
Language thick and vibrant. Drawn to-
a connection she couldn't understand.
A beating drum creeping consistent rhythm
Sending message from the friendlies,
"your existence is incongruous. A path
will be carved on the granite ledge, with
a fall for the green a thousand feet below.
A poem about munificence of assisted death.
The injury was her definition.

From the culture of disability, we
touch the earth's crest in a different way.
The answer is we have always been its lover,
Even when it precludes us from its glories
while we watch from our unique lonely tower.

Ree

An Equal Choice: Why My End

Why *my* end? Choice or force?

 rain on step

cold face

shelter house awaits

pharmacy rejects

landlord leaves toxins

palliation homecare house repair

     denied

        Better this than to be extinguished?

Euthanize or medically assist …. suicide?

Suffering situated in the Euphemized?

To exterminate

or automate autonomy?

escape inequality given to my life less worthy?

So I *die*?

An Equal Choice: The Talon Tip

they came,

nurse, doctor assessor,

precluders of moral penetration

weapon on fingertip

pausing at the mud bank bed to enjoy my movement

then plunge the taloned tipped end.

Sympathy for the Assessor

Today, oh, I saw earnestness, but no happiness.

Aware, a wheelchair and distress I saw

me assessed for death by noon. Strange thing

 a gutted appetite that does not satiate,

where hollow compassion is discourse

for box-ticked patient hidden history

gained by tele-conference analysis.

A promise that your suffering will end when

more billings are brought for people in

the door, or buried in their bed.

Strange thing a business built on backs

of death monetized by what's performed.

Fare for what's tolled to whom they call

 fair access healthcare. An extinguish

now an ethic to inhabit licensure.

An Injection of Ambition

=
==They want
==our people gone,   and they- >
==hold power.
=

Questioning kills careers by those practiced
in medical lethality while
career building committees meet in quiet
until capable of crushing voiced dissent.
A coordination of professional
players; one with a spear thrown as a javelin
to attack a person not their substance,
then in a chorus of victimhood cry in

=
==They want
==our people gone,   and they- >
==hold power.
=

shock with those stealthy actions noticed.
embarrass persons of different views,
prey to over populate committees,
so that they will stay for their built careers,
alienate, humiliate, crush aspirations
open the doors to a healthy debate.

=
==They want
==our people gone,   and they ->
==hold power.
=

Sympathy for the Provider

sliding- YOU shallowly shock the conscious
but still exist to seek a patient

 your back shadow swung full bent
your syringe smiled feigning friend
a crow facing a baby pigeon unfed
a heated swine turned red

It Is Our Fault

Our lonely perch was a granite ledge sloped down.
We, the DISABI-LI-TEE,
are just you and me,
introverts of gratitude,
silent observers of the descent below,
comforted by ramps and posters prescribing charity,
held its jagged wall.
From there we carved a home.
Cut hands on splintered fragments.

They went through the gates below.
Those exorcising difference
with eugenics of euthanasia,
baptized by the power to inject,
learned to state,
'Dignity in death!'
(A sentence sent to sell safe exit
from a care-based jail cell
absent aid to escape soiled sheets)

Misted by vapour on our perch
we slumbered
while the human rights blanket pressed warm.
A quilt of life, security, freedom.
Not vulnerable… not equal

But, the quiet coalescence of
medical triage meat chart
did not rest until the legal test
tipped to death,
as our souls slept.

ACT V

Fair Again

Pebble Made Round

What is forgotten is sometime found
Ignored by the shore,
 a pebble made round

The Pebble

I

Breathing is a straw.

Today…

        I go,

It hit head to shoulder

pressed throat slipping hammer in a downward spiral

holding my chest low

negotiating its departure

But the liquid rattle rolled

ordering tongue eyes cheek to gift air

bacterial splinters owning my long gasp

II

(Alone wheeling over fallen leaves I feel peace)

III

I will find you while on Queensland beach.

At the edge of surf that gnarly toe

will touch a pebble.

Remember when that happened? The toe? We were Jacques Cousteau. (*Plongeurs extraordinaires. Nous etions les petits hommes qui n'avons pas reve judicieusement,* wearing dollar store fins.) You smashed it on the shore.

-I would not have had a real life …

Sans   sans   sans

You

           friend

(I see spouses. That is something else.)

You will be anger and love regurgitating.
End with love.

Find the pebble.

Pub Sweats

Best whiskey is JD Black.

Stone floor sweats

                        piss and bar fight snot.

Travis Tritt on sound.

A lady brings burger.

                        Calls me, "darlin".

                        Kindness and tattoos.

Neck grows with gravity

aged to the downward drink elbow.

exposing honesty.

                        Seems like summer sun just came in.

Light Darts In The Broken Bricks

We/are/people/hidden.
Psyches pressed under linoleum in our shouting
isolation
aware last is last
(evolving white singularity in chaos).
brick buildings of our naive hope
 broken into honeycomb spiers:
wreckage without a broken phone,
Grenade without a pin.

Where do we go from here?
Touch doorframe to feel fresh empty air?
There are light darts in the broken brick
Red door on a restaurant
Swept ice on a sidewalk where no one wanders
a plan inside the cobblestone
moss between the wedges

WITH GLASS AND LAKE VIBRANT BLUE

Emergent from the wind, lightning ripping shore.
Emergent from the Hulkinator homage
shirt ripped pectoral MAGA mental density.
Emergent from airport into sun for taxi
to dream of a belief in location.
Emergent from the chrysalis in
the mix, commencing generational decay.
Emergent from the window.
Emergent into hope balanced on plan planned
intuition returning from redundancy.
Emergent from the gut decayed. An
 intuitive formless loss of Wednesday
punched into a cliff of granite holes
safely, softly, knuckled into rest.

WITH GLASS AND LAKE VIBRANT BLUE

Epilogue

Concrete Creatures

Born on energy from the brown grass mowed
I find walls on a street and no dead end

Walls float on energy where there is no dead end.
Meant for escape we ride on Rainbow Road.

We wander wet riding on Rainbow Road.
I'm a creature on concrete creating a home.

In London concrete creatures call it home,
shrapnel whiskey and goblets of Barolo.

Cut by the Shard where the Globe is low
I see Gloucester's eyes inside Lear's lost love.

With no mother her sauce is tasting lost love.
Penne and sausage bathed in a bowl.

Ending the day where the cricket ball bowls
I'm re-born on the lawn of the brown grass mowed.